INTO THE FOLD

MISFIT

*To Tom —
— who sees things
clearly — hope you
enjoy entering into
the fold!   Jacqueline Turner
            Summer 2000*

INTO THE FOLD

ECW PRESS

POEMS BY

Jacqueline Turner

CANADIAN CATALOGUING IN PUBLICATION DATA

Turner, Jacqueline, 1965–
Into the fold : poetry

ISBN 1-55022-409-3

I. Title.

PS8589.U7476I57 2000   C811'.6   C00-930444-4
PR9199.3.T836I57 2000

A misFit book edited by Michael Holmes
Cover design by Tania Craan
Author photo: Barbara Woodley Cover photo: Roads, Death Valley, USA/First Light
Text design by Jacqueline Turner
Layout by Mary Bowness
Printed by AGMV

Distributed in Canada by General Distribution Services,
325 Humber Blvd., Toronto, Ontario M9W 7C3

Published by ECW PRESS
2120 Queen Street East, Suite 200,
Toronto, Ontario, M4E 1E2
www.ecw.ca/press

The publication of *Into the Fold* has been generously
supported by The Canada Council, the Ontario Arts Council,
and the Government of Canada through the Book Publishing
Industry Development Program. Canadä

ACKNOWLEDGEMENTS

Endless thanks to Fred Wah for sending me off down the line in the first place. Thank you to the University of Calgary English Department for financial support during the writing of this manuscript and to fellow students in writing courses along the way. Thanks to Nicole Markotic and Daphne Marlatt for editorial suggestions. Thanks to Heather Fitzgerald for helping me go into the book, to Karen Robinson who's always willing to explore the domestic. Thanks to my family in Chase: my parents Shirley and Jack, my sisters Sheryl and Lynne and my brothers Randy and Mike and all their families, for unquestioned support. Thanks to filling Station friends along the way who formed a community where there wasn't one before. Thanks to Kate (Arthur) Walters for her brilliant rapport with children, especially mine. Thank you to Michael Holmes at ECW for taking on these triptychs with such sensitivity to how I wanted things to go.

To Bill who sees beyond masks, to Brennan whose intensity inspires me and to Blake whose quick connections keep me laughing: thank you for making this is a good place to be.

This book works because of the work of other writers, particularly Rachel Blau DuPlessis's *Drafts 15-XXX*, *The Fold*, Jean MacKay's *Dragonfly Suite*, Daphne Marlatt's *Touch to My Tongue*, Nicole Brossard's "Image-Nation" poems

Thank you to the editors and editorial collectives of the Canadian small magazines who published excerpts from this collection, including *West Coast Line*, *Tessera*, *Rampike*, *qwerty*, and most recently *W*.

"The worldly, the domestic, the wild:
is this not the very tripartition of social desire?"

Roland Barthes

INTO THE FOLD

Chase chases memories say sand
between toes to start plus a lake, a red
pier and a desire to swimslither cold
(blue water, blue sky) skin prickles
expands again red (that feeling) hair
turning burns blonder still

[insert photo here]

ache edges depth vast and waits wind
winds too cold of a shout offshore
without future lakes in mind

[yearning, fingers, fear]

lake this mountain train track fresh
sulphide fliesfurious (intention always
reveals itself) lost blue against

[ankles, angst]

one hair turn turning

small

Chase chases memories

blank big stop 'run til you puke'
headache breaks easily against cracks

whirling inside 'all you can do' too big
for skin scrapes refuse bones ache burst

blue slaps big boulders water falls
behind desire for just one just one more

yearn yellow of a white car drives
'around and around'

lake lascivious wraps thighs cool bluegreen
almost alone again

Chase chases memories
same as same
water up a nose
flintstone lunchbox breaks
tongue rips cold metal
swings taken again
scratch: snack stolen
purple banana bike seat
red tablets:
how to brush your teeth
jumping the high stair
backs broken crack

1

Shuswap lakes me log cabin lemon
legs stretched deck fresh and big air breezes
slink on a too hot hafta go in baby's heard
againlanguish up

wave to Dad delivering the mail

rocky beach water sooo warm you wanna
sudden deep dives cool but not so
scrape against rock again and air

keep an eye on B in inflatable penguin

vast grass up the hill: rocks and feet heavy
arms failing penguin falls blows back down
B even redder than before kicks head back
tired slides stubborn sleep aside

Shuswap lakes me on the last day of school
boats a two-four with N and S
J and her bikini weren't allowed to go

N knew he'd work on a golf course S
probably didn't know he'd try to kill himself
later seems like the right word water glinting

got going real fast and we'd stop suddenly
and jump in pee in the lake in the clearest
body of water in Canada fluid the water we
knew our skin

S's little sister starts crying drank too much
she wants to go later on the lawn by the beach
she tells me she was pregnant once believes i
won't tell anyone and i don't until now

waves turn foamy white blue cold to my car
water falls against rock on the ride home
contemplate a nap and what's for supper
walkman drowns out the broken stereo

gazebo Dad built for the wedding
(like he said he would)
plastic swimming pool plastic slide
bare toes hair curls still
really big tomatoes
aqua boat + purple skis
bathing suits on the freezer
long, long drives

Kamloops calls pulp mill
fresh says don't stay too
long but "Sahali" offers
something desert dry drive
and drive

stuck in the back singing
'who were you talking to'
unseatbelted bends and
bends alone again river
moves "cell by cell into
a realm unreal" and trains

Call Kamloops "your friend's in the
hospital" psyche ward
again but only organic
brown duster busted
joint in the Plaza parking lot
bright light promises/threatens
hot legs on saturday night
slip between river and lake
fresh black cold
yellowline as

picture w/ Santa —
she looks like a boy!
yeah
almost asked:
can we stop for a hamburger
too afraid felt
inside the chest
we passed it
banging the window
why what

3

First my dog got hit by the school bus, my brother shamed me into not crying, into saying no big deal, into making the bus driver feel better, like it wasn't his fault. Then my new running shoes ripped at the seam, no money to buy new ones, flap flapping around school. I was cautious, waiting for the next thing. Then one day i started crying, hiding in the school washroom, missed the bus home, i couldn't stop crying. A teacher came in to see if i was okay and i said please leave me alone and she did and still i cried. All the way to the bank where my mom worked, crying up the street, my head down, pretending i was invisible over the creek, past the Legion, the mini-mall on the corner, to my mom and i said please please take me home.

Today Blake bashed his head on the hockey stands, crying in my arms, the red welt forming across his head. Today it turned bluish-black. Today Brennan was bugging me, hanging off me while i was trying to get ready not listening to my get out of my space rant and as i eased him out of my way he tripped and fell against the edge of the bed. His recriminatory you pushed me, pushed me past the edge of guilt, his forehead red and swelling would turn purple before we got to school driving silent and heavy. Today i whacked my head on the edge of the van getting in to do up Blake's car seat misjudged the headroom a red line across my head, a headache moving down my spine, oh man i said.

if she always looked like a boy, wanted to be a boy, in fact, pretended to be a boy said don't tell the other boys i'm a girl, if her best friend is a boy, if she always has friends who are boys, if she was always called a tomboy and never wanted to wear a dress. if her hair was always short, if she played with trucks, if she rode a boys bike, if she wanted to be like her brother. if she wanted to be a truck driver or a fireman, if she thought she could escape, if she said girls can do anything they want

too large for frees a forgetful lull fingers pulse against sting lists and list 'what to get'
stretch in the reach among days dog tired and crying pressure pushes low clenches
drop baby drop plexus flex smooth amidst the wide yeps a stammer mmm errrr

rain sings an almost wet, dripping (the you on the screen) slips finger long and still
weighs heavy now beyond the wrong green stems purple here flakes relief of off
stark still and waiting water breaks beats a flow towel soft wave rises tight again

tense in the too much tense release spins back stack wanting ease, sand sun nooo
clench the end of 'this is it' move and move more driftive almost snap spine push
slide rip elide slip pours and pours sent sentence release again ease the yaw of you

Thompson river rides by me sand bar
rising 'it looks like he's walking on water'
and i believe himsea weed wade my way out
current flows around my black rubber boots
hands reach sand cold water fresh wind
ripples the edge laughing, dancing

later when my dog is hit by the school bus
he says 'look, she's going to cry' and i don't
just to spite him and i still don't teeth
piercing tongue and goldensparks

when i think 'm' distant and bad 'how
come he gets to and i don't' knowing it's
because i'm a girl somehow not wanting to
be tree climbing safe

M slap shots the china cabinet shatters
scissors break and rages a broken .22 stuck
between yelling and nowhere to go

read his letters from Sask. - she likes him but
doesn't want to say all the you remembers
and we miss you railroaded he doesn't go
back again

stakes a place drinks a remembering says now
'i wanted to go' his everything was fine sticks
sharp against anger

yellow school bus every day
mom hits the ditch againlate
'why do we have to stay'
wagon wheel for lunch
dog's old rose
giant tree
dirt

Sorrento stares stings an 'i want you'
smooth skin caught almost there push
pushing slings a finger long stripes a
remembering arms long and 'it's late'

drives a haze down talk talking talk
sent singing blood-like snaps a lapse
sent flying

(more exciting than 'the real')

after 'you said he kissed you' docks
sway water breathes us sucks a scape
'until your boyfriend came'

*make a mental picture

presses down on 'have something to
tell you' syllables shake down around
the 'you' of saying

another K, not you

Sorrento starts way down scales rallies
anticipation felt driving legs quiver not
knowing veins swell felt as yearnings

your 'only in town for the weekend'
echoes past ways of committing
(fingers on paper)
to the 'like it'

lakes shimmer too much Monday

black and raining

eyes bounce yellow caught short
shifts 'all' the way (home) staring

highway
gas station
houses
trailers
(he discovers your clitoris)
trees
grass
sand
lake
dock
boat

Scotch Creek skips a beat slides past the
khaki in provincial, the red in park black-top
smooth all the way to the beach

she's crazy about him, but doesn't like us

suntan oiled and sinking sun sand melts a
disconnection (stopped listening, that's all)

beach towel breezes sand eye grit behind
another beer caught wanting waves again

and wet

watch the people go by holding hands
bikinis or not: coupled a frame again waiting

Scotch Creek skips a beat laughs cadential
around curve your arm his arm mark a
note left hanging hugs the heavy bass\

stop short right turn and he's not good
enough for you small against wanting

window of an arm, a head pressed all you
can see
green apartments across the high school
(juicy fruit gum your sister used to live there)

quilt by the campfire
sparks fly fresh
press up a mountain, a moment
tense turn turns forward folds
wh weeps knowing

ripple chips
beer, but don't let the wardens see
trees
rusted barbeques
washrooms and change rooms
garbage cans everywhere
(her hands on his back)
swim out to the dock

He gets his first phone number from a girl: Molly 253-354. The girl he carpools with is his friend from preschool he doesn't remember saying then, she's so beautiful. Older boys tease him recess in the playground, you were riding with a girl. He argues with his friends who say they don't like girls: what about your mom, she's a girl. When i tell him what gay means he says, what's the big deal about that. He is waiting in his room for his time to be up, sent there for hitting his brother. He is waiting, it takes forever, and none of his toys seem appealing. He tries to draw a picture but can't snaps the pencil in half slamming it across the desk. His time is up, but he won't come out. Sitting in the crawl space between two rooms his arms wrapped around his legs. He won't come out. He is not crying by sheer force of will his eyes are closed. Slumped asleep he is found after lots of calling carried to his bed, covers pulled up to his ears he dreams of fighting bugs trying to attack him, dark circles under his eyes when he wakes up.

She has words she likes, particular ones she fixates on, throws into every conversation, tests them plastic in her mouth, can't resist the repetition saying them again and again until someone says, wow you really like that word you use it all the time and fine, she won't say it again, the word will never again cross her lips burning being found out. Ashamed someone noticed they were actually listening when she assumed she was invisible, temporal, flighty somehow above this inane chatter, clutter, clutch of people talking about nothing, the women picking their kids up from school going on about the need for manicures. She really has nothing against manicures except as a topic of conversation along with television that other great topic of talk about she could scream her silent response, she really could. Not one chance to say unctular or portent she probably made it up anyway.

She fascinates traces shape of curve of ever expanding flesh, everyday outward pushing, sets camera on tripod documents growth every three months, the profile stretching black and white frame runs her fingers over improbable skin, lifts the weight of dancing naked in front of the mirror, she finds herself exotic wants to say erotic, lightly moving out to here, nothing fits don't you find me so she says, legs tight bend to squat practicing she breathes deep pictures ocean waves of the blue blue, a touch from behind, a hand on a shoulder curve of back yes she relaxes wet pressure, yes i find you

breezy in the no nausea zone lifts an ambilvalence sleepy and soft-boned stretch
slips an ellipse inbetween times and slow whhh of a deep pillow fresh shiver
moves lightly across hand pressed 'actually feeling' link skin water skin insistent

outward imperative fleshes a presence sent flying lies here now every ache a yearn
touch says stretch tight tips weeping willows against the window wind howls warm
motion again firm mattress caress questions of (o) soft slow www throb thrumm

blurry and outside a lot, talk about doesn't reach remembering in 'what it's like'
left incongruous slip between belonging slog exhaust fumes snow slow of thigh
finally fresh test again (fine) time and time week after pounds appropriate gain

Salt Spring slips wave upon wave sucks
sweet of a baby's breathless breathing wraps
circles again blurs bright eye of it salt wet

*send a postcard to K says she's pregnant

let down ache blue ocean greenscrambles
smooth rock faces purple star slime red
sleepers kick and blackblack hair

        (runs circles around)

flow slips sweet strong pulls and pulls
(take a picture of us) held close closing
in and off

                                                        Salt Spring slips

journal blue jeopardy and comfortable
yearning one glimpse of D. or P.

paper ground glitter black bark

arbutus red peels caught again bruise
bite playful shock

late blurs almost awake asleep grit
together tiny head in hand and on

you say sleep pillow soft until crying

                              lotsa long slugs
                          blue back pack tips over
                               leaves wet
                        crayon drawing of ferries
seals (what looks like kissing each other)
                              broken moped
                              pulley basket
                           crabs, starfish, etc.
                             wind in hair

Savona kills K's brother slides fast black
and gone his friend too probably sleeping at
the time whenbluffs meet black ice: the irony
of 'deadman's'

just pain

same with D on his way to Adam's Lake
either a truck or a red car definitely a red car
when i saw him last smiling

beige phone says: 'dead friend today'

erases/maintains/erases/freezes/

that one moment snap shot fresh and
laughing

E cries when she unexpectedly sees his picture
their daughter living somewhere else but she
can still visit her and gets lots of pictures with
the parents they chose — at the funeral with
her new parents 'she looks so much like him'
wonders why everyone's crying she knows he's
gone but not for how long

K says it only hurts in waves that pass
through the body ending in anger without
screaming seared to the skin blocking

H doesn't know about going to the funeral
her new husband might get upset erasing the
traces she stays home and it rains again goes
to work in the distance cries the black phone
'i should have'

still a young body vs. a physic who says you
know there are no accidents and wow what a
choice screams against

badminton racquet
grade six soccer (goalie)
she said "sweet"
driving gold bracelets
the first time they had sex

Salmon Arm slides second shop Saans
ugly new shoes dance toward wedding
flowers (not as promised because it's too
hot) sips chocolate beans w/ new writers
crystal formflakes

*Elaine's has new Marlatt $14.95

purple castles rise balloon fresh and run to
keep up/keep track B wants one and i
always say yes bored for hours

pick up:
        – eggs
        – milk
        – bread

drive winds hours around 'getting there'
yellow line divides lake/mountain see cows
and (plug your nose) pig farm fresh beside
bumper boats now

Salmon Arm slips less than always makes
you feel sad yearn to be somewhere else

whispers across waves lap lap lap laughing
head back blonde hair brazing the nape

cake calls birthday partysweet from shore
linking arms wishing to walk up

wet towel cold darkness draws us shadowy
we sing softly listen lightly

feet against rock and stars

one big collection of old cars
one old one room school house
(one person still remembers going there)
no public beach access
only Co-op for miles
one traffic light
(mom gets her license there)
six second hand stores
(W laughs about that)

C takes a limo from school there

She starts talking really fast, starts slurring her words together blending and skipping over. Thinks she should stop, but has another glass of beer wedge of lime and carries on louder. Today she is seeing what she can make happen with her words, watches them bounce off the corners of the smoky room music bleeding all around. Asks for a cigarette even though she has never been able to smoke, not even in high school blue bathroom door swung shut, when she really really wanted to. She takes a drag chokes back a cough and continues on about wax dripping waiting for the offers of. At some point she becomes conscious of a line being crossed, some wrenching in her chest, thinks about going home and then lingers past it. Some wanting. Redraws the line perfectly in spilt beer on the table, wipes it away.

There's a gouge today in her ability to get out of bed. She is gouged to the bed. The bed is holding her in its gouge. She is unable to ungouge herself. She looks at the clock, knows, it is time to get up. And yet. This gaping gouge. Caught in the fold, the inbetween. Not sleeping but unable. Caught. The bed — her. Stuck she can't say. Seeping somehow, slipping lip to pillow.

i was so tired up at three breast feeding, up at five again dreaming of sleep, this is some kind of torture i kept saying not again he's crying you should feed him, maybe he's not hungry i say, have you thought of that. i can fall asleep like that now, talking on the phone, in the car, sit still for a second and i'm out. why pretend otherwise, can't think straight, can't remember what we were talking about anyway, my breasts swell into the next feeding lips and steady steady eyes wide and staring

starts with an ache back straight sensation, a mark a dot brackets breaks bigger still
knowingness links uterus flesh dug deep back an ache starts push particles something
gut clenches ambivalent breasts ache both wanting and not slakes tender bones expand

impossible flying feels across the you desires 'the safe return' what's not been lost
keeps and keeps streams a thigh veins trickle...skin between all surface mostly depth
deep linger ache stretch felt here side pulls inside all outside lakes form fresh strong

too slated destiny and soon, let it be soon, space pushes inward licks into shapeless
walks and walks breaks light apprehension of wrists risks not seeing the you of her her
happens again walks circles repeat slide down backs thighs still swims kicks desire

Magna Bay makes me red wharf long
looking for fish (bread on a safety pin) he
naively hopes can't stay still long anyway
yellow wagon yips rock hard hill hangs up
helping

lamenting lake today when B was young
(that kind of nostalgia) pictures in boxes
and not albums

criptych longing white boat on shore lags
for a second lingers the edge left lapping
pullsaway

*B gets up at 5:30 a.m. again

drawing against tired pencil shapes a blue
book rains hard 'a famous blue raincoat'
just want someone to carry the groceries in

lonely sting of 'no one to talk to' slaps a grey
phone unanswered again

even breezes

Magna Bay makes me red wharf longing
sun snapping always waiting for someone
to show reading a really good book at least
the best the bookmobile had to offer saturday
and thursday at 'the store' *The Beet Queen*

Magna Bay slips between my fingers lake
water fresh the edge of remembering his
toes in the sand or small stones skipping

sears an almost onto my forearm, the back
of my leg left kicking glide where you/he
kissed

slipped the purple driveway-fell hard
(out of my arms) grass stain green his head
lip sticking and crying

blue blue purple irises
bluish scotch pines
blur colour finger paintings
vines trail
(lots of water or the grass turns brown)
dandelion fresh
S's horseradish invades insidious
slips cut waiting

Celista swings winds and winds between
lake/rock on the way dances a rock jump
signed in black letters $15 or $25/couple
(band+dj) stopped, hoping to press

singled out wow frog fresh against wanting
waves signal a let down wound around
                                    crying

*kept the ticket scrapebook safe

slip me a
                    caught sighing but cool

the talk about doesn't mention this

dance as phenomenon rare and unsatisfying

(lying trying sighing)

no room for 'this is and is not'

yip yipping reach rawing red

sent shimmer linger off ffff

purple purple flowers
tall grasses
trucks, jacked up
see the black
just stars

Logan Lake lips ellipses between drives
wind mountains for hours to get to the 'new'
immediate laughter lingers a second moves
sleep here floor rises up to meet the edge
of 'stop talking' next room to whisper
swa . . .

laughing again mornings, afternoons swept
left out against quiet 'Dad's sleeping' mine
shift solid still the new is everywhere

links a he and he here school picture fresh
mysterious she hyphens me a remembering
he's soooo but i

lips alliances sent candy store skating waits
for the perfect panel and back spins skips
'all the way up the hill' trips blood stain
beat scraping the new 'wow you're lucky'
lifts and lifts

Logan Lake leans bright and shiny, never
sunny cold lake wind and windy sands 'us'
over edges of wanting to toe poised

(we have never been kissed by a boy)

labelled lezzies wrestling the schoolyard
learning not to hold hands

intense says simple or extreme arms around
pillows first bras digging in snaps a lapse

caught sighing but cool
hair pulled back
slacks back sleep

same striped sweaters
(they look like sisters)
pink bubblicious
Grease soundtrack tape
writing paper
school pictures
purple, not pink

Yearning for sophistication from her trailer bedroom brown panel walls thin enough to have a conversation with her sister through, she always thought if i had the money i could have the best clothes, the coolest wardrobe but now that she does have the money, she still wears the same things just more of them. Her 'i will never live in a trailer' translates itself into a house on a quiet street, not in a small town, her mother's all that money and still not happy echoing through her head. She knows money can't buy happiness, who doesn't, but a great pair of shoes full price gets you pretty far down the street. Despite having lots she wears the same ones over and over. Insidious repetition. Contradictory impulses ripping the fabric red.

Her hip escapes caress wound around a musical embrace arms swinging and high above her head. She knows she's being watched but pretends she doesn't. Her white t-shirt moves up to reveal the stripe of her belly the edge of her jeans her hands move across the air around her waist. If her body was said. Hands on her back now fingers through her hair. Folds around stopping. Sitting on the edge of the couch. Waiting.

sleeping you say shhh even though he's already asleep perfect
pose of perfection soft you pull blue knit blanket over bare
knees begging yourself not to take this moment for granted,
grey haze light your eyes, narrow rest your arm, your finger at
the edge of his cheek, his hair breathe breathe in the palm of
your hands, would kill anyone who touched him now or ever,
fingers curled around the pine bars of the crib reluctant and
tired you turn, negotiate the sharp edges of plastic toys, kick
past a pile of clothes, white t-shirt now and sleeping grey
flannel sheets

way of wander, wonder flipped past oblivious set off fine blur breaks blue wash out talk
kept silent wise stare and stare 'what's known' here hand, back of head fine fine fall llaa
latch crack careful flannel linger scent flying press intense candle low breast stem matters

pillow wise wrapped around dawn nebulous blur blink crimp lip wide wait whhh on
nipple slip passive size electric flow wow rush flux exxx says stammer yow water lick
kick side ellipse wide drift torrent 'off to' shimmers slow way ache cadence in out our

rang again dark white tell langour rise whhh eye even still 'star bright' back skin now
with thrash wound deep praxis heart tepid depend awe every yaaaah yaa all liquid
dedicate flavin normal lamp paper 'written on the (his) body' how if ache capsize

Turtle Valley lulls her sweeping hills trim
distant cows and canner fruit jars tips a
location fought for her version of 'here'
said 'family' and they all listened

water glistens grass drops a second little
tongue fresh plowed over apple tree grass
rising dust and 'now you can't even see the
road' snow says you don't even know who's
coming on the phone again

her 'come over to my house' expands the
walls of comfort cinnamon bun warm
waiting stretches all you can do, still
farther bakes her 'she is soo busy'

first time they road an escalator

Mom touches an electric clothesline and dies
her don't wake Mom and Dad sleeps with
me flannel flowers lower bunk

Turtle Valley trips us dancing freeze frame
fresh the three of 'us'
one long striped
pregnant + two not
we decide 'Brennan'
laugh like dancing girls
rocks the edge of longing to be together
dark and stars we sing slendor skinny

slakes a fall rock caught not crying
too tired against wanting to stay
slips tender shoulder
perfume sweet

watching her orange and black skirt
cheerleading practice
sign really does say 'turtle crossing'
fielding horses
first day of high school (crying)
cat's eye glasses
her own phone
paper thin trailer walls
skip rope turning

Squam Bay scares her drives for hours
logs miles after mile to keep 'it' straight
learns Spanish yearns against gossip

creates a reading of isolation book after
book (neighbours keep coming for coffee)
she negotiates interuption drinks, smokes

leaning to say 'close' cared what she
thought wrought wrung-out and following

wisps blonde wind and blue blue eyes (she
was always the smart one) letters from
Nelson and a crocheted cap from her
roommate. i write: i lost another tooth

i know she likes strawberry yogurt (but not
this kind) and white cream soda, not red
or beige.

sometimes she scares me wine bottle shawl
and cool, so cool always a boyfriend to die
for

Squam Bay takes her city to lakeside
wonder why would she staring across blue
logs a winding road, turn at mile 24
dust drives the edge: cliff, trees, water
pull-out, hoping to hold on to
gravel not giving way

C's first birthday winding
we made it teddy bear cake and tea set

slips between refusing not to go
the 'staying in touch' seems important now
still no phone she tells me
writes about her little red shoes,
her she says, but 'only when she wants to'

alone in her voice
howls between us
slips icy

her cowboy friends
beige firebird
her own apartments
really great clothes
books
green coffee cup
sleeping in

Brennan Creek burns hot day orange
dust creases desire of shoulder bent
throwing baseball hard ache of 'it'

*rewrite the grammar of angst

all you can do drops away rain shower
fresh mud rising up between
slips a finger nailsharp
possible sensations,
positions a perfect response (thought up
ahead of time) felt between shoulders
crease curves a release left laughing off far

the 'you should haves' and 'cared what she
thoughts' slip sunlight anxiety turned right

and leaving

Brennan Creek trips the long way of 'riding
up in the back' dust flies furious obscures
the look of 'it's just fun'
knocks elbow + side of truck
kicks around again winding spins
fingers into backs of hands
beer bottle cool
dances the hall tonight

'beautiful' view of the lake
logging trucks
polyester baseball shirt
basketball in the loft
one room school
coats in the hall

she keeps watching the train go by. she is hearing the train go by. the train goes by her room at night paper thin walls. she has never been on a train. she knows the sound a train makes when it goes over the ties in the crossing. she knows exactly when the bells will start, when the engineer will whistle and how long she can hear the train after it passes. she knows how to count how many cars the train has, how many engines in the middle and what the caboose sounds like. she knows if you put a penny on the track it will get flattened, but if you put too much stuff on the track the train guy will stop and sweep it off and yell at you where you're hiding. she knows the shape and feel of the rocks at the edge of the track, knows they are hard to walk on. she knows how to jump on the train if it's moving slowly enough and how to jump off. she knows her brothers ride the train into town, but she only rides for a few feet. she worries about being sucked under the train becoming a war amps kid

if i cried when my sister came home because she didn't spend
enough time with me, if i got upset because the yogurt i
bought especially for her was the kind she didn't like, if i was
too sensitive, if i couldn't take the slightest bit of criticism, if
i thought her asking me all the time if i had a boyfriend meant
i had to go find one, if she said she liked Iron Maiden even
though i know she didn't, if she came to my grad party, if she
could pass for one of my friends, if she left home before i got
to know her, if she always existed far away, if i planned to cash
in my bank account buy a bus ticket and go live with her, if i
couldn't be that dramatic even if i was exploding inside my
own head, if i was in such pain, if i had known the word angst
if she had said you're okay how you are

slowly she catches the big red ball rolls it back and again he keeps repeating patterns elaborate routines exactly the same arms reaching to throw it just the same way, red ball scraping green green grass until suddenly he stops, moves toward the swing, fingers around chains, kicks little legs higher under to the branch of the tree, touches the back of his neck, tips back hair flying and laughing, she leans against the tree, eases into the back and forth, the shimmering hair, the red ball rolling under her foot

scatter reckless tri wave vacant toes, small toes september wise eyes wide 'remember'
faculty flavour ambiguous of the late, late taken smudge skip over lapse segue green
nine side known glance salad of romance same sentiment finger handle linger mingle

catachresis rises stretch 'kept waiting' gap back can't careful lament straight for second
deep in the hazy hazy yawn wide mist quiet intention navigates awake side down
north of shimmer heavy ready step parcel so long gravitates heart muscle melds up

park tread divide you and buzz line find dark yeps stammer cry still edge fever rate
exact temperature mediates temple lead dist song side elevate possible rake esk card
depth surface wide of the cool, cool submerge angst be belong gather skip layer pale

Chase Creek braids broken down barn
around sandy sandy water picnic scratches
carried along by the current wound back
again feet against rock kick kicking can't
stay strips the cool

sleeping over (culture of girls) tumbles sex
talk and stuffed animals taped over shocking

her 'I can't believe you said that' rises up
toward wanting it tipped back and laughing

(halloween she always dressed a hippie
headband and long long hair)

her dad talks crazy but we didn't know he
was an alcoholic until now slamming hard
black pavement breaks and breaks out

tender to say it her babies now growing
bigger married and 'all' basement economics

shooting lapse between the then never
seen as normal

Chase Creek keeps us LP hippie-like longs
illucid two hands rising wrought out
not crying

eyes flash dirt roads for signs of

'he's cute just invite him over' too terrified
to speak nothing to say spins and spins

surfaces of what if he times infinite

*shy people over-monitor their environment

(don't want to be seen as)

spirals inward chest tight
taped shut and stuck

the coolest ski jacket
her sister's boyfriend
french braids white blonde
first time we saw a condom
smoking in the bathroom
out with J 'forever'

Niskonlith blue blacks the word 'reserve'
our party of passing through wept the other
side of racist by not caring

yellow gold fires edge of the lake and not
wanting to get kicked off quiet music
blares the solitude of a jeep, a tree

fields and fields of wild flowers — here.

night rocks the turns of who will show up
dust hides anxiety anxious felt as clench
hand in the gut

drinking our way to

yaw at the moon yearns a touch but doesn't
say it moves a finger in the dark, a neck,
the back of an ear, leaf entangled hair,
haaah you can see your breath thh

Niskonlith changes us wanting to be sooo

yellow celica drives
the edge of tired of almost

burning algebra notes to signal the end of
erase this we create
another version
fingers black
hair tangled

grab backwards twist twisting
we say 'resist' but

fields and fields of wild flowers
trees out of rocks
fire on the edge of
lake the colour of
dirt smell of
fingers through hair
purple the air

Adams Lake whirls us water speaker blares
inner tube scared whirs to the pulled under

beer cans in the sand

slurps the edge laps between sand and wave
water barely moving now arch of a foot
packed in sand scrapes sweet low

whips around air 'who's there' jean shorts
of the expected frayed but not waiting zips
black bathing suit fresh shakes hotter than

thin, thin white

rips nail sharp: tree + skin jump jumps ridge
fancy silver water shock drop off

falling, but caught

T. always said cold

Adams Lake lifts us slaps surface, depth of
shoulders pressed against water skin
between sand and air hair strands fly wide

waves the current of K. always says almost
lost his license hitch hiking to fastball
games

his tall and blonde hurts against 'playing
around'

perpetually stung finger aches rips the
clench of the 'can't have'

hips press rock grass aches
stakes a second

beer cans in the sand
Boy Drowns in Local Lake
orange life jacket
black bathing suit
frayed jean shorts
zipper stuck
car speakers

drinking by the lake she dances near the fire around and around until somebody worries she might fall in. in her dream she trips against the edge of the rock and falls but wakes up before she hits the fire, startled on the black leatherette couch that came with the trailer and smelled so bad for the first month, something about the glue, that can't be good for you, raking the red shag carpet she remembers the dream the smell of the fire singeing her hair

In her dream she is deciding whether to have sex with the man or the woman. She can't decide. She and the woman send the man out to the laundromat next door. He is back too soon. Says he feels left out. I don't care she says you guys decide. In her dream she hopes the woman will win. The man sulks out i'm not sticking around for this her initials engraved on his shoulder (probably tattooed, but in her dream engraved seems like the better word). The woman turns to her. For a second she thinks about calling the man back, wants to make him feel better. But in her dream she does not.

tracing the space between fingers, the lip of thigh, her hands
starting to go slack, she reaches to turn on the radio music
smooth, but her desire is wider and her angst plays itself out
on her hip, the smooth of her stomach marking the wrinkles
between counting them one by one, she had not thought
alone but wasn't disturbed among choosing reaching again
slender

treble of left cleft tick syntax wrap pour around dying glimmer rips shimmer tied tight
tipped right tremble legs shake ethereal arms around almost tea sipped tepid deliberate
ripple size say tidal relentless lick one last kick cadence sticks smooth quick release ease

zag gone ribald dipped in or out talk a high note shriek keep caring rubbed right here
effort anything but apple lists drink after render how to assemble; what doesn't work now
whether under or tipped top side ellides slender carpet tender burn neglects stream

mama or mom margin wide electric stops eclectic cream sips steam met left wanting
green overwhelms contradictory fingers stroke kept count analogy of toes talk treble
effort falls semiotic crackle forgotten amniotic cycle several lack caves in rose red sable

Field flattens out the sharp side of 'mountain'
railroad crew fresh and passing through his
leaving home lags among tall grass, a desire
for a shower

tops out basketball orange and black frenzy
next quits tips learning side cash wide
teaches me to drive

*does not exhibit the typical characteristics
of a drop-out

pester the tall friends trying to get to the
'everybody likes him' letter C we danced
(nice, but shy i think) kept still shimmering
shy yeah

shoulders wide and tanned span distances
between the we've never actually hugged
scissors flying rage 'the two of them never
got along' left me lonely sent back can't talk

Field takes him backroom to morning train
track flat he weaves among blue, green

hates it, just hates it dirt and sun

arm pinned 'i squealed like a pig' his brush
with the almost intimated on the rye side of
scared

pinched tight he doesn't say sips a Sikh free
Legion drink

kept quiet until the 'i'll never be like him'
rage
caught out, but building yellow siding fresh

train gang, not chain gang
keys locked in car for days
not your typical drop-out
basketball, baseball, golf
matching necklaces
'really in love'
piling lumber
reading Tolkein

Pritchard plexes sexism of x relax last
you say 'fantastic' R. says 'realistic' kicks
knowing from

my yellow yellow

listening to journey expanding space
between fingershighers gravel road don't

yearns a touch makes 'it' happen shoulder
to shoulder hoping to press empty, purple
shell spent relent taken a back came over
here sheer of hip pine trees sway sap stick

cats lick the butter

ponds horse-like away rock fallen not
laughing grey trouble/knees shake stiff w/
the word daughter

'she would'

Pritchard dances ranch house M out-of-town
around trying-on, fixing the broken

calves continually being born blood
late-night dying not knowing the smooth

this we know lightning sharp

panic cure at the start of
always full in the end

food for weeks gone
get me spent
beer bottle refund

party after party
horse riding before school
green tent
boy passed out on the deck
2-4
'her' abortion story
cosmo magazine
the best of journey
'the' 40 acres

Duck Range roams the flat fat greened
flappin seams dirt desperate w/ stalk edge

looks out: vast etiquette of valleys

signals a 'growing up' milk wiped a lip
plagued not knowing 'what's appropriate'
here hand flexes knee, glances inside thigh

thick blonde spills edge of glass ear-lobed
arch of foot + metal ash tray traces cigarette
proper yahhhing lip bitten radio spanning
beer bottle dense to the always after

laugh talk er smears commentary sneer of
the 'i can't believe he' hey tough stuck
closed can't say

warning: trespassers will be prosecuted
(she always thought electrocuted)

Duck Range roves over seems forever wraps
us green going down snow slows a trace
slip started cling curve corner rip stated
gravel ways save a second thinking Cohen
house in the desert 'nobody's wife'
whipped between the 'here' and the 'now'
worn-out laugh skin sheds paper
signal say what

terrible, terrible

phonic remembering slaps a syllable
table top brown
prefix of suspicion
partially accused of

scent of can't say soft rrrrrents
even if i
wa

zap of grass on electric fence
gravel road
first time we drove
'more than a feeling'
top of our lungs
green
not many ducks

i am walking on the sand bar have waded through weeds and reeds to get here to swim on the clear side to be swept along by the current for a ways sand between my toes. i am walking on the sand bar looking for driftwood Brennan in rubber boots finds an interesting piece with a hole in it and says the water is too cold to swim. i am walking on the sand bar swam through weeds brushing my les to my brother who i thought was walking on water incredible i think wow that you could walk right through the middle of the river green of the reserve the tangled trail up the hill arms around my legs watching

playing basketball she says put on an all-Indian line and we'll
kick some ass and she calls her racist says, how can you say
that, sitting on the bench again ball slamming her hard in the
chest when she moves up the court orange and black mesh
shirts flying, what the hell you trying to prove. later when
three girls from the team are pregnant she's not warming the
bench so much, they're not winning much either, sweat
stinging her eyes she drives her home across the bridge past
the reserve church where the playschool is, says stay on the
pill you don't want to, whispers what can happen in secret
with no one knowing remember i said i was going to a concert
that weekend slipping her fingers into the waist of her jeans

You never quite get it right. Bake all the cookies you want, buy a shiny track suit and sit in the hockey stands but no, you're holding back. Your wanting to be seen as, plays hard against not wanting to even be one. The La Leche League meeting where you can't quite commit, breasts aching trying but endless giving and meal planning eludes you and all the things you can't teach your kids. Sure you rationalize, say you're just doing the best you can worry arms wrapped around two boys lying in the big bed waiting for the strength to just get up

swell sets left tip tender render flannel lament kept count June side ever if crisp wrap
pink about taxi last crinkle cast table this label parka wide divide seeps you side my
yellow yammer (fits between, among?) young, young gad drink careful yow slip wow

whether scarpe meant tomorrow worry one more your beat now wanes sensitive verve
echo signs rhyme again nerve after scafold deep layer figures sonic cryptic care within
knowing line blue after rip up stiff stuck capture rapture gape gutteral tape electric six

scape scene skin wide remember slack sings suture seams sorry stitch story you of bring
gave if ever sleep to resemble lent image rage fact of fabric rip red lip to pillow slips
solid crave soft escape pends resemble laud a cell skip over mal land door after root

Blind Bay captures us tomboy free boat
riding our own risk smoke steady sand rise
between foot step

forgot my bathing suit wet pantiesshort
seams dig in

reeds brush back: 'the sand is slimey!'

kangaroo-hooded don't tell them i'm a girl

passed the marina skipping, bike riding raw
between short blonde hair hemmed my oh
ah yeah, sure

slipped our imitation to the power of
hammers, nails, dirt bikes, scrawny trees
of the disapproving suburb

D. sent crashing (no one around to watch)
rode brave before no one no be back by
sky blue, sun orange (yellow?)

Blind Bay backs us forward playing or being
our skin and sand we know
voiced and poised ready to

taboo between us/the reach and the telling
after
saw the same video on V.D. in health class
dancing unhappy

plastic truck drip drops fire 'experimenting'
toxic
play between idea of and skin pushing back
somewhere obliviously beautiful
almost a

can't *afford* a t.v.
yellow waterskiing rope
bikes
the gravel pit
white Spanish-style stucco
cliff jumping
scrawny cedars

Silvery Beach shimmers just simmers
slope talk hot to the red canoe fingers press
paddle side smooth, warm more than across

she dives wharf side says, 'it's okay if you
go out with him' misstepped stroke after
stroke came up crying tree line and sand

deep in clear eyes wide fingers spread deaf
rings loud eeee intense strap slips glimpse
round and perfect to purple surface

escape rhythm-free electric skin bangs on
outside sun and sun on 'all day long' flicks
fireside stone ring

*postcard pretty she lives

sand recasts the alphabet for me; grammar
of a single grain tense between finger nails
scatter there

Silvery Beach stares the edge of purple
eyelash caught torn around the corner

risks sticking speed boat cool
wave after
wrench raw after
extracts back blue
still shakes

flags a second glides smooth so
'the water's like glass'
spray edges lean
hands tight
slides

that red canoe
those grains of sand
that long wharf
those cedar tree lines
the cool water
those postcards never sent
that wooden paddle

Squilax lingers as inbetween vast topically
dry rises out of the old store brick of railway
building red grated floor hurt our feet
candy stick bottle colours milk glass jars

Dad pulls off the highway buys honey from
a family

at school the grimey son says 'you bought
honey from us' and my trying to ignore him
fades a buzz through fracturing friendships
'you bought honey from him' seeps denial
shame-faced

sharp says what falls between us

Squilax band members get new houses 'boy
are they ever lucky' and even though we live
in a trailer we have to feel sorry for them
because somehow we're still better off than
them 'but mom, they live in a house'

imagined confusions of the 'what goes on
there' elides the why

subtle separations — the vast inbetween the
all this the all that

what's possible here: the word 'racism' never
spoken drunken jokes everything's fine here

meeting the anthropologist studying the
reserve i was shocked 'why here why them'
hit with the not like — heard the word
'problem' running to the white washed
church and back

band jobs pay well but nobody wants them
those kids get their entire education paid for but
they won't go

rip your stupid mainstream strip: realizing
the culture of

she rides on the back of a motorcycle through the hills to Ville Franche, thinks she is making a romantic picture the wind in her hair she is not wearing a helmet, this waist her arms tight, this black black hair, if they fall she will be killed but obviously she doesn't care wrapped as she is in this romantic image, the coast below and the winding winding road where every bank statement seems irrelevant, she imagines riding a bike with a basket on the front to the market travelling from France to Canada to visit her family, looks up the word pregnant in her French dictionary, the bike stops at the top of the hill leans off before him runs his fingers through her blonde hair ·

what we thought was a good party depended on the proximity to the lake and the chance to go swimming when we were wasted, although we never did because we were too wasted and it always seemed too cold. it depended on the size of the fire and who was there and who wasn't and how much beer was available and how fast we could drink it and who got together with who, who possibly could get together with who and who could make it happen. we worried about too many trucks coming and too many cowboys and about getting caught, getting kicked off and the cops coming. if we kissed someone it was most probably someone we didn't go to school with, although it wasn't always the case and then we had to deal with saying hello to them in the hallways and it was all too awkward, better to avoid and try to have a conversation on the phone without all the pressure of everyone watching. we thought a good conversation involved some talk of the meaning of life, something deep and profound and also talking about other people we knew if we thought we could seem better than them somehow and also an admission of how wasted we were to make any kind of connection seem inconsequential. we thought it better to not show that we cared what anyone thought although obviously we worried about it constantly, wrote secret entries in our journals speculating what they thought about us

You are so hot have never been this hot before driving through Pacific Northwest heat, no breeze off the coast, no air conditioning in the jeep, no place to put the roof if you took it off, your body a furnace already seven months his hand sticky and heavy on your knee, chewing ice take it off you snap leave me alone, but you're stuck in this jeep with nowhere to go until you get there, your hair sticky and tangled at the back of your neck and lifting it up or tying it back doesn't help, you could give birth at any moment, technically, it would be expensive though and you wonder what ever made you want to be pregnant in the first place, didn't know you'd be this hot sweat trickling now between your tender breasts, would take it all off if you could, would shed this sweaty skin for a moment of cool, for a breeze in the lush early morning grass, would give anything for a dip in the ocean for the shock of a cold water dive in the lake first thing in the morning

excise lax slim numbers ramble evidence emerges slipped or pushed drag guys impossible
ever stretch checks wild wide skin extends beyond fold after tissue tight drape electric
tingle gropes down again heard as rage joined drastic kept delicate triage go one by

yellow fields snap flowers around crowning ying monitors yang gong steady beep
prolong garish push shock hair air rings criptic almost crying grab brought close
even since slick caught tepid dark tendril finger soft rockets sky blue sing say yeah

hey of yawn notion deliverance same stance only more so silk skin drips milk careful
lull saken never so almost awkward division slept toward vision screen on almost you
unify stretch across softer release rip placed together render relax into still slender

Vernon reaches right-hand page of angst
tempts potential lake-side lavender pressed
between

i just want some time to myself

backs of hands peel off known, a hip escapes
caress if my body was said phone book
weight, yellow

touch to my

smooth of a stomach skin and skin slips by
un-done vast of purposeful white spaces
signifying

as so

parchment eyes tear mark to mark wrinkles
line memory of smooth strain theory track
ache of back

calla lily white stretch arm's length of scent
spilled out knowing nihil text sunken ink
of statement

Vernon nexts un- into slack shoulder fact
back by back presses an ease left long

calculate: vertebral degeneration

inside bend relates elbow tight narrates a
missed glance, skips past save

v of hand curves a draft spelled out here
hip paper flex dyed black by

cantya just

space between fingers
lip of thigh
uvula

Copper Island dives fusion scalp wide
water and blue, blue air of neck snaps back
bathing suit black

i have never loved George Bowering

rock between rock and feet on the edge of
poise, of almost; lurch and then

fast spray splash swoop back curve up
relax fresh rush surface seems so

caprice seizes shoot wide so green shrub

Copper Island hikes the wide side of scape
seeks similitude of view, of look

D. says 'jump' and eventually

(legs crossed again)

climbs lip side scrapes bend of skin felt
here back of knee sinks well fresh

*well above sea level

motor boat gasses water green, purple
slick behind the eyes blue and glassy

rock
cliff
flower
water

Jade Mountain surveys highway wide
infinity of view wow of the always loved

gas jockey job

green but not so curves anticipation slender
lens a sunglass flash temple smooth

i'm driving in your car

wind say waaah air through hair after hair
glass elbow line when

turn on the radio

pictogram graffiti red D. K. + R. L. forever

yellow yellow yellow yellow yellow yello

rock flies

Jade Mountain mesmerizes almost
anticipation felt here fingers grip smooth
smooth wheel wrapped around press

purple to say it, not green really

lake me tree waiting for
alley after alley home
free for a second hair whipped back

interior render
scene snap fax

push button car radio
dark red impala
windows mostly rolled down
grey dash
almost out of gas

staring at wheat fields listening to Cohen sing nobody's wife, she is struck by the vast transformed into an unbearable ache she cannot bear, jumps the fence tramples the canola that used to be called rape seed, picks handfuls and smells them tosses them into the air, she wants to dance through the fields but can't get over the absurdity, kids staring at her from the back seat of the car, she knows they want to keep going to get there but all of this driving in a straight line makes her slightly crazy, sincerely L. Cohen the song flips around she is back in the car driving crying the kids say okay mommy and reach for her hair tangled by the wind fingers tight around the steering wheel, now Sheryl Crow sings a change will do you good

Today you will laugh more throw your head back in careless abandon. Today you won't care what anybody thinks throw your arms to the wind drive all the windows open. Today that ache in your chest won't drag you down won't stop you from, won't make putting your arms around a tiny head such an effort. Today you will say the first thing that comes into your head, blurt babble out at random cackle see the words crackle fly fling your hands going along not stuffed in your pockets not today

The kids are screaming in the van hitting each other and
calling crybaby when one or the other cries, so i start out easy,
calm and in my best parent voice say, please be quiet boys i
can't drive with all the noise, he hits him again and i scream
stop, so they both start mimicking stawp stawp and laughing
and now they're not fighting but i'm so mad flashed back to
my brothers teasing me go tell mom why don't you rage and
humiliation these boys i say don't quietly

ring one place you knew water wrinkles rivers slake steady thirst ready easy or red dive
extra almost strands swap around low wavers seem simple every yip yaw wants schwa
aggravate each hassle felt slack capable slips around back cables simple what seams to

open nectar original lake effort tops sloppy slip of messy sent out back care easy every
yes sips sweet table top ponder risk of cake exclaim matter ruby fruit terrible slunk
kennedy or good dexterous snack kip called with us smack cracker friend deep para

agate ponder smooths rounder slips under ram dirt side danger red scar rakes tissue often
no not ever rambles sent together stone heavy level labour til time takes tomorrow sweet
sorrow wanes scent fresh side shovel lip stick catch change phrase frenzy zag gone swallow

Seymour Arm shore wide wakes sandy
isolation slips noxious impossible nation:
audacious colonial action built up the lake
and back

boat wide hauling kept edge tugboat steady

lilt of hammer echoage amidst: rock, then
gravel, then road then lines edges landscape
frenzy and wow what a big

(we also drove up grape koolaid for mix)

logging trucks lean high long wide red flag
trees a discontent sand pressed pedal

Seymour Arm marks a scar
leg against tent peg
tree uprooted here
pinking lake water
my brown brown
'you're bleeding' wasted
dirt beneath fingernails
fuck first aid
shallow hole

generator power
tent pegs
one manor
lunch trailer
a marina

Vancouver skates the S—curves of long
longing salt sea sushi green squished blue
and then white of an eye caught gazing
slip fingers pull

to feel what you see

breezes crease skins inhale burn white nails
of a summer sun mango fresh flesh stains
orange of a summer sun sets palms aglow
and wow your hair feels kiwi green and
black seeds slip stick finger

what your tongue hears

licks waves salty splashes snap sandy feet
squishes grit of rubbing so loud your teeth
ache vibrating a crescendo swallowed too
fast a flick tongue crashes hard on white
enamel

inhale with pores open wide

lying the air holds whirls 'round and round'
sinks a wet wind sucks every drop salt
embeds light embues the embrace of caught
waiting again

sea wall mermaid
slick acting classes
sand swinging
drive for miles
writing *schools*
separate pillows

Monte Creek has a crush on me won't
leave me alone anymore always asking me
to the next dance red faced no no he'll just
ask again next time

moves me i should be flattered and if you
look with the corner of your eye but no you
can't everybody watching your response

starving for affection one arm around your
shoulder holding hands but not that one

Monte Creek leans tallest boy in grade 10
against my locker pleads behind me walking
to class ignoring him for show

sits behind me on the bus hand on the back
of the seat shy lingering lapses into blank
stare nothing to say

if i say tree after tree hi howareyou if i turn
toward the back of the bus if my hand brushes
lunch crumbs off the metal part of the seat

what to do when the wrong
guy has a crush on you

how to say 'no' without being mean

how to find a real boyfriend

what boys want in a girl

Sunset she's looking at pink says if you painted that it would be tacky, ocean calm and breeze wood of a clapboard chair seals bobbing, she remembers cold mist north sea her grandmother's brother, father lost at sea waiting waiting she moves west to Saskatchewan prairies and apparently never misses the sea, the wheat moving across the prairie in waves, forgets her girlhood Georgina by the sea, running along skipping, she never went back never wanted to, cutting peat black like pudding, she never wanted to, swimming on the one warm day of summer sunburnt she serves dry toast without butter and tea, strong tea sun on your breasts the first time you suntanned topless côte d'azur release into eyes closed deep slipping sleep rendered you are your own, drawing arm over head the morning, the afternoon, not moving deeper into sand of the blue blue, nowhere to go for the moment, ease of a silent thought about nothing grip of a kiss, side of neck toss of hair shoulder bites, arms length tongue and nipple of seclusion felt here or here, you are slack wide sensation slipping lip to tongue walking down the road by the river faster but still walking thinking ahead of myself, driving myself i am wondering why did i and what do they think now and why do i always and if only i could and then the sky fragments blue triangles in front of me and i'm walking into a Picasso landscape, hands my hips now jutting at awkward angles, my eyes leap ahead of me, green prisms of field hurtling the bright all rolled up behind me now, giant colourful i am running now, staying ahead scattering parts of myself as i go dispersing the worn pavement

BEYOND TONGUE

'would you know proposition
if it kissed you
on the back of the neck?'

arms wrapped around
here or her fingers
stuck yes or shy

why don't   you call   just talk
erase the trace of kiss   \voice
trembling almost crying

her 'she said i kissed you'
slips among
your dancing with him

if her kiss
is hard
and his soft?

miss a beat lip wide
slow skips
water merges fingers

amniotic stroke
scent eventual flow
stride the wave of belly

whirring he says proud
(she too loud)
wonder stuck-on lip stick happy

walking the halls
stop to puke
disconnect back of his hands

her arms around her shoulders
do you mind soft
kiss pressure base of spine

licks what the tongue
staves off
outside a finger touches lip

home to him on the couch
eases into that too
large kisses lips everywhere

smitten among skin
newborn soft stroke
tiny arms flung around

necks of the always loved
pulled-in cheek to chest
quiet across thighs

you suspend
ambiguous breasts
him or her or him or

slip past labels
or into
mother lover wife other other

risks her mouth wet
weighs fingers
marks flesh

fold after fold after
her flexible extension
wrenches which fingers

cherub cheeks
they look the same
they look like you

agony of choosing
drinking to decide
always wanting somewhere else

white silk around potential finger
like your father you
can't say

red of playful flesh
wet surprise fold after
holds your tongue tight

not trembling you wear
green flowers lavender
look at poetry as if

her arms around her shoulders
suspended breasts wanted
ambiguous lips

body of obsession
you felt the overwhelm
stings smartly

or ever the narrative
of fingers through hair
kissing the rising slack action

both the boys
you love
still wanting

her arms around her shoulders
fingers through her hair
she wants to kiss you again

nape of neck
torn here
rejoined, threaded

you refuse to regret fingers
hands play out
curve of her back

fingers manipulate, extend
you never simulate embrace
abrasive edge

brush back black hair
black of black dark eyes pool
reaching eyelids

(except for seeing he chooses not to)

littler eyes still
stare intent fingers
stroke your face

white t-shirt raises
eager mouth to breast
relaxes flannel body

too tired dreams of sleep
he wakes loud
slips in quiet

trickles wet shirt, sheets, bed
over produces swell
linger cold toes to warm

flat out
improbable fingers
tiny reach

swollen easily twice
its normal size
crisscross stitches

vulva wow
stretches steady
yaw of him and him and

inner and then outer
literally, you said
entwine finally i said release

he rubs your
fingers wide prying
lifts your hair twists to the nape

(when you finally
get enough sleep and
can have a conversation)

carry on skipping remember
grabbing for a finger of thought
you read

and it comes
eating kiwis
with spoons

fingers around
back of her
nipples slip

turning her lips
rolling into your mouth
over your teeth and tongue

bite between neck and shoulder
arms raises
tender before elbow

lick
breasts
to jut of hip

hands clasped
or released
moving

repetitive
her arms again
fingers stuck yes, or shy

rising heavy
you have   what can she say
to go torn   to make you stay

flowered stress
button up blue
she fingers fabric

orange of
he loves you
fingers striping white t-shirt

rake of red back
he was expecting you earlier
you say   here   (at least)

careful wrists
wrapped in silver
some symbol

resembles you
especially with
his helmet off

if we were too
cynical to believe in
seeking the unconditional

fingers wrap wrists
he slips into the curve
your body   again

she dances the edge
holds your tongue in her mouth
moves from yes to no to

cool wrap sheets or
surprise of flannel fingers
or

still rising writhing
sheets around ears
gouge the bed

finger tip to nail
press until you feel yourself slip
tend towards you

farther from ear
lobes sucked to her
perfect perfection

silver rings in some
other language beyond
tongue

placate my desire
flick of lip
you could say   wanting

over ringed finger
rapacious lust
like holding

your tongue in his mouth
dances she's watching fingers slide
over voyeur

smack a red ass start
led delicate dread so
far ruined but stung

grapple me a rhythm
smooth steady toward her leaning
already framed view

wherever you say   when
asked beer after and so
on kneads you an increase

waking with those other hims
into your clasping fingers
holding perfect

feather not one regret sneezes a release
launched full speed into morning
you say hmmm high voice non stop

one by one they edge together
slip sideways off the bed run the stairs
who gets there first

tip right side left
together
keep going

scared felt below the ribs
(who gets where first)
one by one this is
troubled by inevitable fingers